You Might Be in a Country Church If...

By Ron Birk

ILLUSTRATED BY DAVID ESPURVOA

LANGMARC PUBLISHING • SAN ANTONIO, TEXAS

You Might Be in a Country Church If...

by Ron Birk
Illustrator and Cover Artist: David Espurvoa

Cover Graphics: Michael Qualben

© Ron Birk, 1998

First Printing: 1998

Printed in the United States of America

PUBLISHED BY LANGMARC PUBLISHING
P.O. Box 33817, San Antonio, Texas 78265

Library of Congress Cataloging-in-Publication Data
Birk, Ron.
        You might be in a country church if-- / Ron Birk.
            p.   cm.
        ISBN 1-880292-23-8
            1. Rural churches--Humor. 2. Country life--Humor.
        3. Rural churches--Caricatures and cartoons.
        4. Country life--Caricatures and cartoons.   I. Title.
        PN6231.R87B57   1998
        250--dc21   98-28123
                                                                              CIP

INTRODUCTION

According to my dictionary, the word "country" has its roots in the Latin word "contra," which means "opposite." It refers to "the region lying opposite the cities."

That definition is helpful in understanding people who live in the "country." In many ways they are the opposite of those who dwell in the city.

Urban people who live close to each other, who labor indoors with careers in the corporate world of industry and technology will naturally have a different outlook on life than their country cousins who reside in remote, wide-open spaces and work outdoors in the independent business of agriculture.

The same holds true for churches in rural and urban locales. Athough they may have a common Lord, subscribe to the same doctrine, belong to one family of faith, the perception and expression of belief can vary greatly from Servant of the Streets Church, Big City, USA, to Shepherd of the Fields Church, Country Crossroads, USA.

This book is an affectionate attempt to present some unique characteristics of the country church. It contains observations from one who has deep rural roots. As far back as I can trace my family tree, all my ancestors were involved in farming or ranching and had at least nominal ties to a nearby church. That kind of heritage has not been lost on this current-day rancher and church member. I have great love and respect for country people and their churches.

My hope is that what follows will be a mirror in which rural church folks will see and celebrate themselves, as well as a window through which city church people can come to a better understanding and appreciation of their country cousins.

So wherever your particular pew is located, just kick back and have a field day grazing through this book. May it feed your soul and cultivate a smile.—*Ron Birk*

YOU MIGHT BE IN A COUNTRY CHURCH IF...

...THE DOORS ARE NEVER LOCKED.

You Might Be in a Country Church If...

...the Call to Worship is "Y'all Come On In!"

YOU MIGHT BE IN A COUNTRY CHURCH IF...

...WORSHIP THAT BEGINS AT 8:15 A.M.
IS CONSIDERED THE LATE SERVICE.

You Might Be in a Country Church If...

...MEMBERS COME TO WORSHIP EARLY

SO THEY CAN PARK IN THE SHADE OF THE TREE.

You Might Be in a Country Church If...

...BY THE FRONT DOOR THERE IS A BOOT SCRAPER.

YOU MIGHT BE IN A COUNTRY CHURCH IF...

...THERE ARE MORE MEN

WEARING HIGH HEELS THAN WOMEN.

You Might Be in a Country Church If...

...IT IS LOCATED MORE THAN 25 MILES FROM A "RESUME SPEED" SIGN.

You Might Be in a Country Church If...

...ON THE WAY THERE YOU GET THE FEELING
NOAH'S ARK CAME TO REST NEARBY.

You Might Be in a Country Church If...

...THE PASTOR IS OFTEN REFERRED TO AS
"THE PREACHER."

You Might Be in a Country Church If...

...The Preacher needs a
four-wheel drive vehicle to visit members.

YOU MIGHT BE IN A COUNTRY CHURCH IF...

...YOU CAN SIT IN THE PEW AND HEAR
A COW MOO, A GOAT BLEAT, OR A ROOSTER CROW.

You Might Be in a Country Church If...

...PEOPLE GRUMBLE ABOUT NOAH
LETTING COYOTES ON THE ARK.

You Might Be in a Country Church If...

...IN A STUDY OF THE OLD TESTAMENT
THE COMMENT IS MADE,
"HEY, IF THERE WAS A TRIBE OF LEVIS BACK THEN,
THERE'S BOUND TO HAVE BEEN
SOME COWBOYS AROUND, TOO."

You Might Be in a Country Church If...

...The Preacher says, "I'd like to ask Bubba to help take up the offering"—and five guys stand up!

You Might Be in a Country Church If…

…ITS ZIP CODE IS E-I-E-I-O.

You Might Be in a Country Church If...

...THE PHONE NUMBER USED TO BE "TWO LONGS AND A SHORT."

You Might Be in a Country Church If...

...TO GET THERE YOU HAVE TO CROSS THREE CATTLE-GUARDS.

You Might Be in a Country Church If...

...THE REST ROOM IS OUTSIDE.

YOU MIGHT BE IN A COUNTRY CHURCH IF...

...AT A POT-LUCK DINNER,
TEN OF THE FIFTEEN MEAT DISHES
ARE VENISON SAUSAGE—
AND THE OTHER FIVE ARE BARBECUED BRISKET.

You Might Be in a Country Church If...

**...OPENING DAY OF DEER HUNTING SEASON
IS RECOGNIZED AS AN OFFICIAL CHURCH HOLIDAY.**

You Might Be in a Country Church If...

...IT IS KNOWN LOCALLY AS
"THE COW PASTURE CATHEDRAL."

You Might Be in a Country Church If...

...THE STEEPLE HAS EVER BEEN USED
AS A HUNTING TOWER.

You Might Be in a Country Church If...

**...THE MEN OF THE CHURCH SPONSOR
A TRIP TO THE COUNTY TRACTOR-PULL.**

YOU MIGHT BE IN A COUNTRY CHURCH IF...

...IT SPONSORS A TEAM IN THE COUNTY WASHER-PITCHING LEAGUE.

You Might Be in a Country Church If...

...CARS PULL OVER TO THE SIDE OF THE ROAD
WHEN THEY MEET A FUNERAL PROCESSION.

You Might Be in a Country Church If...

...A MEMBER REQUESTS TO BE BURIED IN HIS
FOUR-WHEEL-DRIVE TRUCK BECAUSE, "I AIN'T NEVER
BEEN IN A HOLE IT COULDN'T GET ME OUT OF."

You Might Be in a Country Church If…

…Members take the pastor's role as
"Shepherd of the Flock" so seriously,
a standard part of the Call is membership in the
State Sheep and Goat Raisers' Association.

You Might Be in a Country Church If...

...THE MEMBERS KNOW MORE ABOUT BEING
A GOOD SHEPHERD THAN THE PASTOR DOES.

You Might Be in a Country Church If…

…IN THE ANNUAL STEWARDSHIP DRIVE
THERE IS AT LEAST ONE PLEDGE OF "TWO CALVES."

You Might Be in a Country Church If...

...NEVER IN ITS ENTIRE ONE-HUNDRED-YEAR HISTORY HAS ONE OF ITS PASTORS HAD TO BUY ANY MEAT OR VEGETABLES.

YOU MIGHT BE IN A COUNTRY CHURCH IF...

...THERE ARE MORE PICKUP TRUCKS
THAN CARS IN THE PARKING LOT.

You Might Be in a Country Church If...

...IT'S YOUR TURN TO MOW THE PARKING LOT.

You Might Be in a Country Church If...

...WHEN IT RAINS, EVERYBODY'S SMILING.

You Might Be in a Country Church If...

...PRAYERS REGARDING THE WEATHER
ARE A STANDARD PART OF EVERY WORSHIP SERVICE.

You Might Be in a Country Church If...

...PASTED INSIDE THE HYMNAL'S BACK COVER
ARE THE WORDS TO HANK WILLIAMS'
"I Saw the Light."

You Might Be in a Country Church If...

...A SINGING GROUP IS KNOWN AS "THE O.K. CHORALE."

You Might Be in a Country Church If…

…YOU CAN LOOK OUT THE WINDOW AND SEE STRAIGHT DOWN THE ROW OF A CORN OR COTTON FIELD.

You Might Be in a Country Church If...

...ITS FIRST-AID KIT IS AN ALOE VERA PLANT.

You Might Be in a Country Church If...

...FRIENDS, NEIGHBORS, RELATIVES,
AND FELLOW MEMBERS
ARE ALL THE SAME PEOPLE.

You Might Be in a Country Church If...

...THE CHURCH DIRECTORY DOESN'T HAVE LAST NAMES.

You Might Be in a Country Church If...

...the Property and Maintenance Committee
has a line-item in its budget for
duct tape and/or baling wire.

YOU MIGHT BE IN A COUNTRY CHURCH IF...

...THREE FEET OF THE STEEPLE IS MISSING
DUE TO A LOW-FLYING CROP DUSTER.

You Might Be in a Country Church If…

…THE PASTOR HAS A PASTURE
WHERE HE RAISES SOME LIVESTOCK,
WHICH HAS EARNED HIM
THE NICKNAME, "MR. GOODRANCH."

YOU MIGHT BE IN A COUNTRY CHURCH IF...

...THE PASTOR WEARS BOOTS.

You Might Be in a Country Church If...

...A CONGREGATIONAL MEAL AT NOON
IS CALLED "DINNER,"
AND IN THE EVENING IT'S CALLED "SUPPER."

You Might Be in a Country Church If...

...THE DISCUSSION TOPIC FOR THE MEN'S GROUP IS,
"WHAT KIND OF MEAT
DID NOAH SERVE ON THE ARK?"

YOU MIGHT BE IN A COUNTRY CHURCH IF...

...ALL THE MEMBERS KNOW EVERY OTHER MEMBER'S
MIDDLE NAME, MAIDEN NAME, AND NICKNAME(S).

You Might Be in a Country Church If...

...FOUR GENERATIONS OF ONE FAMILY
SIT TOGETHER IN WORSHIP EVERY SUNDAY.

You Might Be in a Country Church If...

**...ITS MAILING ADDRESS
INCLUDES THE WORD "ROUTE."**

You Might Be in a Country Church If...

...IT IS LOCATED ON A DIRT ROAD.

You Might Be in a Country Church If...

...THE PASTOR PREACHES A SERMON ON
MANNA FROM HEAVEN USING THE TITLE,
"THE GOD FODDER."

You Might Be in a Country Church If...

...A SPECIAL EVENT FEATURES A TRAVELING COWBOY
EVANGELIST PREACHING FROM THE BACK OF HIS HORSE.
HIS SUBJECT: "THE SERMON ON THE MOUNT."

You Might Be in a Country Church If...

...THE ONLY TIME PEOPLE LOCK THEIR CARS
IN THE PARKING LOT IS DURING THE SUMMER.
AND THEN ONLY SO THEIR NEIGHBORS
CAN'T LEAVE THEM A BAG OF SQUASH.

You Might Be in a Country Church If...

...some "Visitors" are not welcome.

You Might Be in a Country Church If...

...THERE IS NO SUCH THING AS A "SECRET" SIN.

You Might Be in a Country Church If...

...IT IS LOCATED SEVENTEEN MILES FROM THE NEAREST SIN.

You Might Be in a Country Church If...

...The Preacher owns a tractor.

You Might Be in a Country Church If...

...The Preacher has a camouflage clerical shirt.

You Might Be in a Country Church If...

...THE ONLY THING LIBERAL ABOUT MEMBERS
IS THEIR GENEROSITY.

You Might Be in a Country Church If...

...THE THEME FOR THE ANNUAL STEWARDSHIP DRIVE
IS "SHEARING TIME."

YOU MIGHT BE IN A COUNTRY CHURCH IF…

…MORE THAN HALF THE MEMBERS
HAVE BEEN TO A COWBOY CAMP MEETING.

You Might Be in a Country Church If...

...BAPTISM IS REFERRED TO AS "BRANDING."

You Might Be in a Country Church If...

...IT HAS A LOT OF MEMBERS
WHO ARE OUTSTANDING IN THEIR FIELDS.
(LITERALLY)

You Might Be in a Country Church If...

...IT IS WHERE NEW SEMINARY GRADUATES
ARE PUT OUT TO PASTOR.

You Might Be in a Country Church If...

...YOU CAN SIT IN THE PEW
AND HEAR A WINDMILL TURNING.

You Might Be in a Country Church If...

...THERE IS AN ONGOING RUMOR
THAT THE POPE BOUGHT A NEARBY RANCH
WHERE HE INTENDS TO RAISE PAPAL BULLS.

YOU MIGHT BE IN A COUNTRY CHURCH IF...

...AT A POT-LUCK DINNER
ALL THE VEGETABLES ARE HOME GROWN.

You Might Be in a Country Church If...

...MEMBERS THINK THAT TO GET INTO HEAVEN
YOU HAVE TO BRING A COVERED DISH.

You Might Be in a Country Church If...

...PEOPLE KNOW THAT EVEN A LITTLE BULL
CAN PRODUCE A LOT OF SACRED COWS.

YOU MIGHT BE IN A COUNTRY CHURCH IF...

...THERE IS A SPECIAL FUND-RAISER FOR A NEW SEPTIC TANK.

You Might Be in a Country Church If...

...PEOPLE SINGING "BRINGING IN THE SHEAVES"
ACTUALLY KNOW WHAT "SHEAVES" ARE.

YOU MIGHT BE IN A COUNTRY CHURCH IF...

...FINDING AND RETURNING LOST SHEEP
IS NOT JUST A PARABLE.

You Might Be in a Country Church If…

…YOU MISS WORSHIP ONE SUNDAY MORNING
AND BY TWO O'CLOCK THAT AFTERNOON
YOU HAVE HAD A DOZEN PHONE CALLS
INQUIRING ABOUT YOUR HEALTH.

You Might Be in a Country Church If...

...THE PASTOR'S ROUNDS OF VISITING THE SICK
INCLUDE A STOP AT THE VETERINARY HOSPITAL.

You Might Be in a Country Church If...

...THE CEMETERY IS CLOSE ENOUGH
THAT AFTER A FUNERAL SERVICE
PEOPLE CAN WALK TO THE BURIAL.

You Might Be in a Country Church If...

Here Lies Billy Joe
Who Made Good in the City
He Worked Everyday
In the Big Nitty-Gritty
But He Knew in His Heart
One Day He'd Be Back
Thanks to 80 Flights of Stairs
And a Cardiac Attack

...MEMBERS MOVE TO THE BIG CITY,
BUT RETAIN THEIR MEMBERSHIP
SO THEY CAN BE BURIED IN THE CHURCH CEMETERY.

You Might Be in a Country Church If...

...its Youth Group is called "The Yearlings."

You Might Be in a Country Church If...

...THE PLAYGROUND IS A TIRE SWING.

You Might Be in a Country Church If...

...ON A CHURCH OFFICE TABLE
THERE IS A COPY OF
Better Barns and Pastures Magazine.

YOU MIGHT BE IN A COUNTRY CHURCH IF...

...THE HAT RACKS ARE MADE OUT OF DEER ANTLERS.

You Might Be in a Country Church If...

...MEMBERS DON'T THINK TWICE
ABOUT DRIVING THIRTY MILES TO WORSHIP.

You Might Be in a Country Church If...

...NO MATTER WHAT THE DENOMINATION, THERE IS
AT LEAST ONE MEMBER WHO HAS BEEN BAPTIZED IN A CREEK.

You Might Be in a Country Church If...

...PEOPLE TOOTING THEIR HORNS
WHEN PULLING INTO THE PARKING LOT
ARE NOT RESPONDING TO THE
"HONK IF YOU LOVE JESUS" BUMPER STICKERS.
THEY'RE CHASING CHICKENS OUT OF THE WAY.

You Might Be in a Country Church If...

...HIGH NOTES ON THE ORGAN
SET DOGS IN THE PARKING LOT TO HOWLING.

You Might Be in a Country Church If...

...A HEAVEN WITH "STREETS OF GOLD"
IS NOT NEARLY AS ATTRACTIVE TO MEMBERS
AS ONE WITH "GREEN PASTURES."

YOU MIGHT BE IN A COUNTRY CHURCH IF...

...IT'S NOT HEAVEN,
BUT YOU CAN SEE HEAVEN FROM THERE.

YOU MIGHT BE IN A COUNTRY CHURCH IF...

...MEMBERS KNOW ENOUGH ABOUT AGRICULTURE
TO WONDER ABOUT THE BIBLICAL STORY OF
JOSHUA AND CALEB RETURNING FROM CANAAN
SAYING IT WAS A LAND
"FLOWING WITH *MILK* AND *HONEY*"
—AND BRINGING BACK
A BUNCH OF *GRAPES* TO PROVE IT.

You Might Be in a Country Church If...

...PEOPLE WONDER WHEN JESUS FED THE 5,000 WHETHER THE TWO FISH WERE BASS OR CATFISH.

You Might Be in a Country Church If…

…ALL YOU CAN SEE FROM THE FRONT STEPS
IS MILES AND MILES OF MILES AND MILES.

You Might Be in a Country Church If...

...IT HAS A STORM CELLAR.

You Might Be in a Country Church If...

...IN THE ADULT SUNDAY SCHOOL CLASS
THE TEACHER ASKS,
"WHAT DO YOU THINK OF THE INTERNATIONAL CRISIS?"
AND RECEIVES THE REPLY,
"GOOD TRACTOR."

You Might Be in a Country Church If...

...PEOPLE THINK "RAPTURE" IS WHAT HAPPENS
WHEN YOU LIFT SOMETHING TOO HEAVY.

YOU MIGHT BE IN A COUNTRY CHURCH IF...

...WEDDINGS THAT *DON'T* HAVE A
COUNTRY-WESTERN DANCE AFTERWARDS
ARE THE EXCEPTION TO THE RULE.

You Might Be in a Country Church If...

...THERE IS MORE SILVER IN BELT BUCKLES
THAN IN THE OFFERING PLATE.

You Might Be in a Country Church If...

...The Preacher has ever used the sermon title:
"Soul Conservation."

YOU MIGHT BE IN A COUNTRY CHURCH IF...

...THE CEMETERY IS IN SUCH BARREN GROUND
THAT PEOPLE ARE BURIED WITH A SACK OF FERTILIZER
TO HELP THEM RISE ON JUDGMENT DAY.

You Might Be in a Country Church If...

...in the Men's Room
there is a bar of Lava soap.

You Might Be in a Country Church If...

...IT SPONSORS THE LAST "FLOAT"
IN THE HORSE-FILLED RODEO PARADE.

You Might Be in a Country Church If...

...MORE THAN FIVE OF THE FOLLOWING OCCUPATIONS
ARE LISTED IN THE CHURCH MEMBERSHIP DIRECTORY:
CATTLE BUYER, SEED SALESPERSON,
RURAL MAIL CARRIER, IRRIGATION SYSTEM INSTALLER,
STEER ROPER, HAIL INSURANCE SALESPERSON,
SEPTIC TANK BUILDER,
TRACTOR-PULL MECHANIC, FARRIER,
FERTILIZER SPREADER OPERATOR,
BOOT MAKER, OR WINDMILL REPAIRMAN.

You Might Be in a Country Church If...

...THE FINAL WORDS OF THE BENEDICTION ARE,
"Y'ALL COME ON BACK NOW, YA HEAR!"

About the Author—

Ron Birk is a Texas goat and cattle rancher who also spent twenty years as Lutheran Campus Pastor at Texas A&M and Southwest Texas State Universities. "Semi-retired" from the ministry, Ron now devotes his time to the ranch and his career as a communicator.

He has written three other books: *What's a Nice God Like You Doing in a Place Like This?—You Can't Walk on Water If You Stay in the Boat*—and *St. Murphy's Commandments*.

Birk is also a popular humorous after-dinner speaker appearing before various types of groups around the country. For speaking engagement information contact:

Ron Birk
101 W. Mimosa
San Marcos, Texas 78666
512-396-0767

About the Illustrator—

David Espurvoa, Director of Publishing Services at Texas Lutheran University, lends his cartooning genius and humor to make *St. Murphy's Commandments* and *You Might Be in a Country Church If...*"must have" books.

Recently David wrote and illustrated his hilarious book, *The Complete Guide for Over-Protective Parenting*. As an "over-protected" child himself, he sees humor in his own role as a new parent. For more information, contact—

| *Ordering Information* |

LangMarc Publishing
P.O. 33817
San Antonio, TX 78265
1-800-864-1648